CODING WITH

PYTHON FOR KIDS

LEARN HOW TO USE THE MOST POPULAR

PROGRAMMING LANGUAGE IN JUST 3 DAYS

DEVELOPING SIMPLE SOFTWARE

ON YOUR OWN FROM SCRATCH

IN A SIMPLE AND FUN WAY

FRANK NOLTE

Table of Contents

Introduction

What is coding? Coding is the act of writing computer software or the language of computers. When you write software, you're programming your computer so that it does what you tell it to do. It is important to understand that coding is more than just writing code; it's about making abstractions from the existing data in your resources to create a greater understanding of the processes involved and how best to work with those processes.

It is about creating a language that will describe things as they are or could be. It can be hard stuff, but it's not rocket science and you don't need to be a genius at it. The goal is to make ideas tangible and understandable through the use of code.

Although most people who write code are software developers, there are a lot of people who write computer programs without writing any code. Anyone can learn to program in different languages.

Coding can be used for a variety of purposes, from creating websites to developing apps and games. It's used in web development, programming, and video making. It's possible to code any portion of the content of a system on any number of nodes to show that it is related to each of its concepts or categories.

It's important to be creative and to have fun while you code, but it's also important to make sure that your creations are useful and help people solve problems. Programming is a challenging and fun activity, and the skills that you develop through programming will help you in school and work.

It's one of the most exciting and fascinating careers because you have the ability to make something from nothing. I'd recommend trying to get involved in software development. Because more and more businesses are becoming technology-dependent, the demand to know how to program is going to grow. Programming is a really important skill that you can use to boost your career prospects. It teaches you how to think logically, creatively, and analytically by solving problems. You can leverage your skills and knowledge to build a product or service that solves a problem people have.

Programming can be a great way to showcase your creative side and help you think about problems in different ways. As a programmer, you must go out and learn new things. The ability to do so is inherent in your job description as a programmer.

The ability to create or build something from nothing is a fundamental life skill. Whether you're an entrepreneur, developer, writer, designer, or creative director, the ability to create something from nothing is the key to success.

This book focuses on basic programming concepts and gives a great introduction to what it's like to be a programmer. You'll have a good understanding of how the technology works and what it takes to build something new.

If you've always been interested in programming, or even if you're completely new to it, then this is the book for you. Anyone that wants to learn how they can make a career out of programming should read this book. This book is aimed at kids, but adults can also use it if they are working on the matter for the first time. If you're not familiar with software programming (and builds), it's a great place to start. It explains Python in a very easy way for everyone who wants to learn the language.

Python is a great language for people who want to learn how to code. It's an easy language, and it's very flexible and easy to understand because of its syntax. It also has a high level of abstraction that makes it powerful. It is one of the most popular programming languages, so there are lots of resources available to learn it.

As a developer, you'll need to build software that you or your clients will actually use. To do this, you'll need to understand how the software works. It's important to understand software programing and avoid depending on the applications available on the internet. It is also vital to understand what goes into a build, before you get started with it, and how much time your project takes.

This book is a hands-on guide that will give you the basics of programming, with an emphasis on problem solving and efficiency. This book is a great starting point. It's an easy-to-read guide, and it's got plenty of examples that can help you get started on your programming journey. The best way to understand the programming process is actually to do/build one.

Programming is an art form and can be a great creative outlet. It is an amazing skill to have, and it's something that will allow you to achieve a lot in your life. Technology has allowed for so many different types of applications and games to be developed, which is one reason why it's been so successful in the mobile app market.

When you're programming, you get caught up in the process and forget that it's supposed to be fun. The most exciting thing about creating something is sharing it with other people. That's the real fun part and the whole reason why we do this. The internet is a place where people go for entertainment. You could help them with a game or application that they can then share with their friends and family. If you're into game development and you're a part of the social media community, then your best bet is to create some exciting social media applications that you can share with other people via the internet. A lot of people think that games are only for kids, but it doesn't have to be that way.

Programming is all about problem-solving and being creative. It's not a task to be done in a monotonous fashion. Programming can be a great job and very rewarding, but it's also important for you to remember that you should have fun irrespective of what you do and be very passionate about it. You'll enjoy it more and you'll produce better results if you have fun doing it. If you are in love with what you do, it will be easier to stay motivated.

DAY 1: Principles of Programming

Chapter 1: What Is a Programming Language and which Are the Most Popular Programming Languages?

Programming Language

A program is a set of instructions (also known as a computer program) that tell a computer how to perform certain tasks. A program can tell the computer what to do when to do it, and what data to use as input or output. Then, a programming language is used to create the program to instruct a computer on how to perform specific tasks. There are many different programming languages, but they all have the same fundamental purpose of being able to instruct a computer on how to perform particular tasks.

Which Are the Most Popular Programming Languages Now?

Nowadays eight popular programming languages are being used extensively in the programming field, are "C++," "C#," "JAVA," "JAVASCRIPT," "PHP," "PYTHON," "VISUAL BASIC," and "HTML."

C++ Programming Language

The C++ language is developed from the C language.

The C language was developed by D. M. Ritchie of bell LABS in 1972. It is not designed for beginners at first, but for computer professionals. C is a process-oriented programing language. When the scale of the software development projects increases, C is no longer suitable for the needs of computer development. It cannot handle complex and large tasks.

In this software crisis situation, C++ language came into being; it was developed by Dr. Bjarne Strostrup, from AT&T Bell LABS in the 1980s.

The C++ language

- is compatible with both advanced and primary languages
- has excellent portability (simple and easy to use)
- supports for object-oriented programming
- can handle large and complicate programs
- has fast compilation speed and development

C# Programming Language

C# is an object-oriented, advanced programing language developed by Anders Hejlsberg and his team of "Microsoft." It is a secure, modern, simple programming language derived from C and C++. C# is particularly suitable for software development under the ".net" framework. It was designed to combine the high efficiency of "VB" ("Visual Basic") with the power of C++. C# supports rapid program development, doubling the efficiency, and freeing programmers from the tedious, repetitive work of programming. It has a perfect design makes it a wise choice for new programmers.

The C# language

- is a modern general-purpose programming language.
- is easy to learn.
- is an object-oriented language.
- works on ".Net" Framework.
- can be used to develop high-efficient programs.
- is programming by using components or modules.
- is easily readable and maintainable.

Java Programming Language

The Java language was invented by "Sun Microsystems" in May 1995. Java is an object-oriented programming language. It has two characteristics: Powerful and easy-to-use.

The Java language was developed from C++, so the syntax of Java is similar to that of C++.

Programs written in Java can be widely used in personal PCs, database centers, game consoles, science supercomputers, mobile phones, global cloud computing, and the internet. Java has the world's largest community of developers and professionals.

The Java language

- is developed for the internet but makes security a top priority.
- can make web pages come alive.
- can change web pages from static to dynamic.
- can block computer virus transmission.
- can produce small applications (applets).
- breaks through the machine environment.
- once written, run anywhere.
- can run across any computer platform.

JavaScript Programming Language

JavaScript is a web programming language. It is a dynamically typed, prototype-based language. JavaScript is part of the browser and is widely used on the client-side as a scripting language. It is used to add dynamic and interactive functionality to web pages. JavaScript is abbreviated as JS.

JavaScript was first developed by Netscape's Brendan Eich on the "Netscape Navigator" browser in 1995. Netscape management wanted it

18

to look like Java, so it was named "JavaScript." In fact, JavaScript is completely different from Java.

JavaScript is a relatively secure client-side scripting language based on objects and events. It can respond to the requests from users and create a series of dynamic effects.

The JavaScript language

- runs with any browser.
- is embedded its code in the HTML page.
- is an interpreted language, doesn't need to compile.
- can make a static web page into a dynamic web page.
- provides form processing and validation confirmation.
- responds to the requests from the user at any time.
- provides an event trigger mechanism.

PHP Programming Language

"PHP hypertext preprocessor" is a general-purpose open-source scripting language. It is a scripting language that is executed on the server-side—a common web programming language.

PHP was first developed by Luddorf in 1995. He began programming in "Perl," then rewrote in C, including access to databases, and eventually invented the PHP language.

PHP is an HTML-embedded language, which means documents ready on the server-side. The language style is similar to that of the C language.

PHP is widely used in the "IT" (information technology) world.

The PHP language

- mix some syntax from Perl and C, which ultimately becomes PHP syntax.
- has HTML code embedded.
- has a compilation that can achieve encryption and optimize the code.
- runs faster than Perl in dynamic web pages.
- supports all the popular databases and operating systems.
- uses C and C++ for the extension of the program.
- can run on "UNIX," "LINUX," "WINDOWS," and "Mac OS."
- can be used to develop large business programs.
- is an object-oriented language that works with "MySQL."

Python Programming Language

Python is a simple, easy-to-read, and extensible computer programming language. And, compared with other languages, it is easier to learn. Currently, Python has four major applications:

- Web crawler
- Web development

- Artificial intelligence design
- Automated operation and maintenance

Python is an object-oriented, dynamically typed language that was originally designed to write automated scripts (shells), but nowadays it is increasingly being used for independent, large-scale projects.

Since the Python language was born in the early 1990s, it has been widely used in system administration tasks and web programming. The founder of Python is Guido van Rossum from the Netherlands. Python is free and open-source.

The Python language

- is very easy to learn, especially for programming beginners.
- is written in C language and runs very fast.
- has strong portability, so it can run on various platforms.
- can run programs directly without compiling.
- can be extended with the C or C++ languages.
- contains a lot of Python standard libraries for various tasks.

Visual Basic Programming Language

"Visual Basic" is a general purpose, object-based programming language developed by Microsoft. It is a structured, modular, object-oriented, visual programming language.

"Visual" refers to the method of developing a graphical user interface (GUI), so you don't have to write a lot of code to describe the appearance and location of interface elements; instead, you just add a pre-created object to a point on the screen.

"Basic" refers to "Beginners All-Purpose Symbolic Instruction Code", is a widely used language in the history of computer technology development.

The Visual Basic language

- has simple syntax, is easy to learn, and is designed for beginners.
- supports visual platforms or regular platforms.
- is programming with components or controls.
- is suitable to develop "Asp.net" projects.
- is easy to convert to C# language.
- has an event trigger systematic included as well as built-in functions.
- becomes powerful with the library "Visual Studio."

HTML Programming Language

"HyperText Markup Language" (HTML) is a standard markup language for creating web pages. HTML was released in June 1993 as a working draft of the internet engineering working group.

HTML can describe and express the web page's text, picture, animation, color, music, event, and interaction. The contents of a web page consist of many HTML tags and elements.

An HTML file has three parts: The "declaration section," "head section," and the "body section."

HTML is the foundation of web programming, which means that the World Wide Web is based on hypertext—a web browser executes HTML files.

The HTML language

- is used to design a web page.
- consists of many html tags and elements.
- starts with the tag <!doctype html> in the html file.
- saves files with a ".html" extension name.
- works with "CSS" (Cascading Style Sheets), which improves the html style.
- is executed by a web browser, which works as a "parser" (a software for analyzing programming languages).

Chapter 2: Why Learn Python?

Python Is Free!

There are no better reasons for you to start learning Python than these: Downloading the program is absolutely free, using Python programming language is free as well, and you can play with it, for free, as much as you want. The language is improved every day by the Python team as well as so many volunteers all over the internet, and so, there is so much for you to have fun with as you continue learning the language. If there is a programming language that you really need to learn, it is Python.

Python Is a very Easy-to-Learn Programming Language

Many people that have used Python agree that it is in fact the easiest programming language to learn. Beginners learn Python really fast, and before long, they are able to use codes and program like experts. The commands used in Python—that is the code that you write—are written in normal English.

Remembering commands in Python is very easy too. You can also easily tell what you are doing and what you need to do. Python is quite different from other languages where you have to remember some abbreviations that sometimes do not make sense.

There Are Resources Everywhere

Python members, as well as volunteers, have ensured that resources are easily accessible for those that want to learn Python. You can get a 'Beginners Guide to Python' easily, for instance, to get started in learning the language. There are "YouTube" tutorials as well, and so many more resources over the internet that can help you get started in learning the programming language.

Great Paid Resources

Most of the resources you will get for Python are free, but some are not free. There are books, for instance, that offer more information and techniques than you will get from the free ones. They have been well developed and tailored to help learners get started and gain the relevant skills of using Python language in the least amount of time possible. You have everything that you need to learn Python at your disposal.

It Is the Language Used in Google

"Google" uses Python; Python is one of the most preferred programming languages by Google experts. Most of their popular products have been programmed using Python. Google is constantly looking to hire experts in Python. If you have always wanted to work with such a great team, Python should be the most important language you should learn. If Google is using it, you can imagine how many more great companies are using the same program, so you are a winner if you have Python skills.

Python Is a Versatile Programming Language

This means that it can be used for just anything, large, small, online, and even offline projects. The skills you will garner will not go to waste; on the contrary, you will find them useful in so many projects that you will be undertaking in life.

It Is Very Fast to Use

If you have used several different programming languages, you will realize that some take some time to program. This is not what Python is like; it is quick to program. Writing codes in Python can be done in a simple manner and really fast.

It Is Always Updated

Python is always up to date, all thanks to the volunteers that keep updating and developing it every day. The fact that it is an open-source programming language helps a lot too since it is open to improvement by a lot of people. New versions are always coming up, and this means that the language is always fresh and moving with the current trends. This is what makes Python a very powerful language that will not fade away anytime soon—it is slowly becoming a favorite of many programmers because of this fact.

Learning Python Is not just Simple but Fast Too

You do not need so much time to become an expert in Python programming language. You can learn the language and be able to use it really fast. If you love computers and are not afraid of simple mathematics equations, you will learn them much faster. Learning Python will not take you as much time as it can take you to learn any language.

Python Has a Great Support System

The great Python community will ensure that you have help whenever you need it. The community members are always more than willing and ready to help. If you have an issue, you can't figure out about the program, or there is a link that you can't find; you can ask for help right away and help will be on your way immediately. The support system makes learning Python much easier, and it makes using the program more fun too as everyone within the community is talking about the same thing every day.

Python Is the Foundation that You Need

These days, programming skills are a requirement for so many jobs in the business market. Employers are looking for people who can program like experts, so those who can understand programming language to understand the data that has already been created by the business. Python is a much easier programming language to learn and so it can help you learn the basis of the programming language you need to know to land the kind of job you have always dreamed of. Once you learn Python, you can master so many other programming languages thereafter.

DAY 2: Introduction to Python Programming

Chapter 3: OOP (Object-Oriented Programming)

Object-Oriented Programming with Python

Python allows several programming paradigms, including object-oriented programming (OOP). The OOP is a way of structuring the code that makes it especially effective by organizing and reusing code, although its abstract nature makes it not very intuitive at first glance.

Object-oriented programming in Python is optional and so far, we have not used it directly—but we have done so from the beginning. Although its biggest advantage appears with long and more complex programs, it is very useful to understand how POO works since this is how Python works internally.

The basic idea is simple. If we have a more complex type of data than we have seen so far as lists or dictionaries, and we want to create a new type of data with particular properties, we can define it with a "class," something similar to a "def" function. Suppose we want to create a type of data called "Star," which will only have one name, to begin with, we can write:

```
# Let's create star.py

class Star(object):

    """Class for stars"""

    def __init__(self, name):

        self.name = name

    # Special method called when doing print

    def __str__(self):

        return "Stars {}".format(self.name)
```

The class has a special main function "__init __ ()" that builds the element of the Star class (called an object) and is executed when it creates a new object or instance of that class; we have put the name as the only mandatory parameter, but it does not have to have any.

The mysterious "self" variable, with which each function begins (called methods on objects), refers to the specific object we are creating—this will be clearer with an example. Now we can create "Star" type objects:

Star.py library that includes the Star import star class

# New instance (object) of Star, with a parameter (the name), mandatory
star1 = star.Star («Altair»)

What returns when printing the object, according to the method __str__

print (star1) # Star Altair

Print (star1.name) # Altair

When creating the object with the name "star1," which in the class definition we call "self," we have a new data type with the name property. Now we can add some methods that can be applied to the "Star" object:

```
class Star:

    " "Star class

    Example classes with Python

    File: star.py

    " "

    # Total number of stars

    num_stars = 0

    def __init__ (self, name):

        self.name = name

        Star.num_stars + = 1

    def set_mag (self, mag):
```

```python
        self.mag = mag

    def set_pair (self, pair):

        " "Assigns parallax in arc seconds" "

        self.pair = pair

    def get_mag (self):

        Print "The magnitude of {} of {}". format
(self.name, self.mag)

    def get_dist (self):

        " "Calculate the distance in parsec from the
parallax" "

        print "The distance of {} is {: .2f} pc" .format
(self.name, 1 / self.par)

    def get_stars_number (self):

        Print "Total number of stars: {}". format
(Star.num_stars)
```

Now we can do more things a "Star" object:

```
import star

# I create a star instance

altair = star.Star ('Altair')

altair.name

# Returns 'Altair'

altair.set_pair (0.195)

altair.get_stars_number ()

# Returns: Total number of stars: 1

# I use a general class method

star.pc2ly (5.13)

# Returns: 16.73406

altair.get_dist ()

# Returns: The distance of Altair is 5.13 pc

# I create another star instance

other = star.Star ('Vega')
```

```
otro.get_stars_number ()

# Returns: Total number of stars: 2

altair.get_stars_number ()

# Returns: Total number of stars: 2
```

Is not all this familiar? It is similar to the methods and properties of Python elements such as strings or lists, which are also objects defined in classes with their methods.

Objects have an interesting property called "inheritance" that allows you to reuse properties of other objects. Suppose we are interested in a particular type of "Star" called a "white dwarf," which is "Star" with some special properties, then we will need all the properties of the "Star" object and some new ones that we will add:

```
class WBStar (Star):

    " "Class for White Dwarfs (WD)" "

    def __init __ (self, name, type):

        " "WD type: dA, dB, dC, dO, dZ, dQ" "

        self.name = name

        self.type = type
```

```
        Star.num_stars + = 1

    def get_type (self):

        return self.type

    def __str __ (self):

        return "White Dwarf {} of type {}". format
(self.name, self.type)
```

Now, as a "class" parameter, instead of using an object to create a new object, we have set "Star" to inherit the properties of that class. Thus, when creating a "WDStar" object, we are creating a different object, with all the Star properties and methods and a new property called "type." We also overwrite the result when printing with "print," defining the special method "__str__."

As we can see, the methods, which are the functions associated with the objects, only apply to them. If in our file, the "class," we have called "star.py" and that now contains the "Star" and "WDStar" classes; we add a normal function that can be used as usual:

```
class Star (Star):

    ...

class WBStar (Star):

    ...

def pc2ly (dist):

    " "Converts parsec to many years" "

    return dist * 3,262

And as always:

import star

# Convert parsecs into light years

distance_ly = Star.pc2ly (10.0)
```

Chapter 4: The Importance of Data Types and Variables

Data Types

Each data type has specific characteristics that enable Python to use it accordingly. For instance, an integer can be used in arithmetic operations. However, the mathematic operations are different if the values have decimal points. This is the main reason why most programming languages categorize their data.

The most common data types used in any programming language are:

- Integers
- Floating-point numbers
- Strings

The table below gives examples of these data types:

Data Type	Example
Integers	-3, -2, -1, 0, 1, 2, 3

Floating-point numbers	-4.25, -4.15, 3.45, 3.14, -1.00
Strings	'a', 'b', 'result', '9 Dogs', 'etc.... '

Remember that both "integers" and "floats" can be saved as "strings." Arithmetic operations cannot be performed as long as they are set as a string data type. To put things in perspective, a string is basically the "ASCII" (American Standard Code for Information Interchange) character codes for the characters between quotations.

Integer Type

One of the best things about Python is that integers do not really have any programmable cap to how long they can be. The only realistic constraint found is how much memory you have on the computer executing your program.

1. x = 100000000000000000000 *12344567890
2. print(x)

Program Output:

```
1234456789000000000000000000000000
```

Python assumes that the programmer will be using a decimal number system by default so it does not require a prefix to use it. A decimal number system is a system that you use to represent numbers by utilizing digits from 0 to 9 and rolling over after. So, in essence, we add another digit after we reach 9 to the left and start counting again. There are other number systems; the most famous being the binary which is used by computers, and hexadecimal since it makes it easier to understand binary.

If you decide to use a different number system, also known as number base, it can use one of the prefixes in the table below:

Prefix	Base	Interpretation
0b (zero + lowercase letter 'b') 0B (zero + uppercase letter 'B')	2	Binary
0o (zero + lowercase letter 'o') 0O (zero + uppercase letter 'O')	8	Octal
0x (zero + lowercase letter 'x')	16	Hexadecimal

0X (zero + uppercase letter 'X')		

To try it out; you can use Python to print out the decimal values of different number base representations.

1. print(10) #Base 10 (decimal).
2. print(0o10) #Base 8 (octal).
3. print(0x100) #Base 16 (hexadecimal).
4. print(0b10) #Base 2 (binary).

Program Output:

```
10

8

256

2
```

Floats Type

The floating-point data type is a numerical type based on the decimal system that allows the variables to have decimal points. There is a built-in automatic function where Python will change an integer to a floating-point in the case that it requires to, such as in dividing numbers.

1. x = 8 / 7 # Dividing 8 by 7.

2. print(x)

3. y = 8 / 4 # Dividing 8 by 4.

4. print(y)

5. z = 8 // 4 # Dividing 8 by four but only retrieving an integer.

6. print(z)

Program Output:

```
1.1428571428571428

2.0

2
```

A programmer can incorporate floating-point values into other mathematical functions. Spend a few minutes going through the documentation found in the link below: "https://docs.Python.org/3/tutorial/introduction.html#numbers"—if the coding you are going to use is math-intensive.

Converting Data Types

At the beginning of programming, when using certain data types can be confusing, in many cases, the data that a programmer needs to use is not really up to them. Data conversion can be a life savior while writing code.

Here are a few examples of data conversion and how to identify the data type of a variable.

- example = 20
- example=int(example) # Changing the type to an integer.
- print(type(example)) # This shows the type of variable you have.
- example = str(example) # Changing into a string.
- print(type(example)) # This shows the type of variable you have.
- example = float(example) # Changing into a floating-point.
- print(type(example)) # This shows the type of variable you have.
- example=False
- example = bool(example) # Changing into a Boolean.
- print(type(example)) # This shows the type of variable you have.

Program output:

```
<class 'int'>

<class 'str'>

<class 'float'>

<class 'bool'>
```

Basic Variables

Any seasoned programmer will agree on two facts about coding:

43

1) Different algorithms can be developed to solve the same problem

2) Different code can be written to implement the same algorithm.

Variable Definition

Variables in programming are based on the variables in arithmetic calculations. Think about them as drinking cups that can be filled with different tasty beverages. Sometimes, we will need to predetermine the kind of cup based on what we are drinking. Although it can be done, it is not wise to drink hot coffee in a plastic cup. When defining variables, it is essential to tell "Python IDE" (integrated development environment) what type of data you are using so that it deals with it appropriately.

When we refer to variables in programming, we say that they are used "to store data" to be referenced and used by programs. Moreover, it is good practice to label them with descriptive names, so our programs can be understood clearly. Remember that their sole purpose is to store data in memory.

This is one of the most challenging tasks in computer programming. Many beginning programmers struggle with finding names that are meaningful and nonrepetitive. Try to always keep in mind that someone else may read your code, so it needs to make sense. That person may as well be your future self, looking for a piece of code you wrote a few months or even years ago.

Naming Variables

Names are case-sensitive, so if in the same code you have "tire," "Tire," "TiRe," and "TIRE," these would be four independent variables in the program. So instead of variables "Looking_like_this" they become "lookLikeThis". Note that the official Python code style "PEP 8" does state that underscores should be used. Regardless, the camel case is easier to type and elegant.

If you are going to work with a team on a single program, sticking to a certain style throughout your program is one of the first things you should agree on.

When you assign a variable, remember these important rules:

1. It can only be a single word.
2. It can only have letters, numbers, and the underscore character "_".
3. It cannot begin with a number.

Look at the table below to find different acceptable and unacceptable names for variables:

Acceptable Variable Names	Unacceptable Variable Names
tire	winter-tire (hyphens are not allowed)

winterTire	winter tire (spaces are not allowed)
winter_tire	8tire (should not begin with a number)
_tire	42 (should not begin with a number)
TIRE	tire_pr!ce (cannot have special characters)
tire3	"tire" (cannot have special characters)

Assigning a Value to Variables

This involves initializing a variable the first time a value is stored. In this example, we are placing the price of tires. While assigning, the best thing to do is to state the following command as 'Putting forty into tires' because the equal sign, as we will learn later, is also used to compare variables.

1. tire = 40
2. print(tire)

46

Program Output:

The output for this assignment is 40, so the program will display 40.

```
40
```

Now, let's try to add taxes to the price of the tires. If you assign a new value to a variable that has already been assigned, the old value is erased—seriously, gone and not coming back unless you rerun the program.

Let's look at an example below:

1. tire = 40
2. taxes= 2
3. taxedTire =tire + taxes
4. print(taxedTire)

Program Output:

In this case, we assign the price of tires to 40 and the cost of taxes to 2. Then we changed the tire cost to be equal to the initial value (40) plus the price of taxes (2) which gives us an output of 42.

```
42
```

In this next example we will copy the value of a variable to another variable, by using the same example above.

1. tire = 40
2. taxes= 2
3. taxedTire =tire + taxes
4. tire = taxedTire
5. print(tire)

Program Output:

```
42
```

Just as we assign numbers to the variables, you can also assign a variable with a string. To let Python know that you want to store a string and not another variable, we need to use quotation marks.

1. tireOrigin = 'Japan'
2. print(tireOrigin)

Program Output:

```
Japan
```

For this next example, we will want to display the price and the place it was made in as an output. By adding the plus symbol between words, it will display both strings side by side.

1. tireOrigin = 'Japan'
2. tirePrice = 42

3. tireOutput = tireOrigin + str(tirePrice)

4. print(tireOutput)

Program Output:

```
Japan42
```

Now that's what a space is: A character! Once you place an addition symbol followed by the space character between quotations, then place another addition symbol followed by the second variable. Look at the code below:

1. tireOrigin = 'Japan'

2. tirePrice = 42

3. tireOutput = tireOrigin + ' ' + str(tirePrice)

4. print(tireOutput)

Program Output:

```
Japan 42
```

Chapter 5: Strings, Lists, Dictionaries, and Tuples

Strings

Strings are essentially a string of characters. For example, words or sentences. In Python, strings are designated by single (' ') or double quotes (""). Just like Booleans and other numbers, there are certain operators and functions you can use in Python on strings.

You can use "+" to concatenate two strings. See below:

```
In [10]:  str1 = 'bob'
          str2 = 'met'
          str3 = 'sarah'
          print (str1+" "+str2+" "+str3)

          bob met sarah
```

You can also change strings to upper and lower case using the "upper()" and "lower()" functions in Python, and you can use the "count()" function to determine the number of characters in a string. See below:

```
In [11]:  str1.upper()
Out[11]:  'BOB'

In [12]:  str1.lower()
Out[12]:  'bob'

In [13]:  str1.count('b')
Out[13]:  2
```

Another useful function is "replace()," as it lets you replace one character with another in a string. See below:

```
In [14]:  str1.replace('o','r')
Out[14]:  'brb'
```

What Is a List?

In "Python shell," you'll input it as "favorite_colors= ['red', 'blue', 'purple', 'green']." You then program your computer to "print(favorite_colors)," and you get all the items on your list as "[red, blue, purple, green]."

You may be wondering what lists and strings are. A list has several features that a string doesn't have. It allows you to add, remove, or pick one or some of the characters on the list. Imagine that over the next few years you decide you have one more favorite color you want to add to your existing list, or you no longer like a particular color. A list in Python allows you to manipulate it.

A string can't allow you to add or remove without changing the entire characters in it. We could print the second item in "favorite_colors (blue)" by entering its position in the list (called the index position) inside square brackets "[]." The index position is the position the computer sees the items in the list. To computers, index positions begin from 0 instead of the regular 1 we're all used to. So, the first item on your list is in index position 0, the second item is in index position 1, and so on.

You'll enter something like, "print(favorite_colors[1]" in Python shell, You'll get blue after hitting "Enter."

To change an item in your existing list, you'll enter it this way:

favorite_colors[1]= 'yellow'

print(favorite_colors)

You'll now have:

"['red', 'yellow', 'purple', 'green']" as your list.

You have successfully removed the item "blue" and replaced it with "yellow" at index position 1.

In this case, "append" adds an item to the end of a list. It goes this way:

color_list.append('white')

print(color_list)

['red', 'yellow', 'purple', 'green', 'white']

To remove items from a list, use the "del" command (shorthand for delete). To remove the third item on your list, it goes:

del color_list[2]

print(color_list)

['red', 'yellow', 'green', 'white']

We can also join lists by adding them just like adding numbers, using the plus symbol.

If your first list includes numbers 1 to 3, and your second list includes random words, you can join them as one list. Here's how:

second_list=['buckle', 'my', 'shoes']

print(first_list + second_list)

After hitting "Enter," you get:

[1, 2, 3, 'buckle', 'my', 'shoes']

Working with Lists

Now, we have obtained one piece of information. Moving to the next one, let us find out what is at the start of this list. To do that, we will call up the first element, and this is where the concept of index position comes in.

An index is the position of an element or item in a list. Here, the first element is "Joey" and to find out that, we will do this:

friends = ["Joey", "Chandler", "Ross", "Phoebe", "Rachel", "Monica"]

print(friends[0])

Here, we will use the square brackets and use the value "0." Why zero and not one? In Python, and in quite a few languages as well, the first position is always a zero. Here, "friends[0]" essentially tells the program to print the component with the first index position. The output, obviously, is:

Joey

There is another way to do this. Suppose you do not know the length of the list, and you wish to print out the last recorded entry in it, then you can do that by using the following method:

friends = ["Joey", "Chandler", "Ross", "Phoebe", "Rachel", "Monica"]

print(friends[-1])

Program Output:

Monica

The "-1" will always fetch you the last entry. If you use "-2" instead, it will print out the second to last entry as shown here:

friends = ["Joey", "Chandler", "Ross", "Phoebe", "Rachel", "Monica"]

print(friends[-2])

Program Output:

Rachel

There are other variations involved here, as well. You can call the items from a specific starting point. Using the same list above, let's assume we want to print out the last three entries only. We can do that easily by using the starting index number of the value we want to print. In this case, it would be the index number "3."

friends = ["Joey", "Chandler", "Ross", "Phoebe", "Rachel", "Monica"]

print(friends[3:])

Program Output:

['Phoebe', 'Rachel', 'Monica']

You can also limit what you want to see on the screen further by setting a range of index numbers. The first number—the one before the colon—represents the starting point. The number that you input after the colon is the endpoint. In our list of friends, we have a range from zero to five, let us narrow our results down a little:

friends = ["Joey", "Chandler", "Ross", "Phoebe", "Rachel", "Monica"]

print(friends[2:5])

Program Output:

['Ross', 'Phoebe', 'Rachel']

Remember, the last index number will not be printed; otherwise, the result would have also shown the last entry.

You can modify the values of a list quite easily. Suppose you want to change the entry at index number five of the above list, and you wish to change the entry from "Monica" to "Geller," this is how you would do so:

friends = ["Joey", "Chandler", "Ross", "Phoebe", "Rachel", "Monica"]

friends[5] = "Geller"

print(friends)

Program Output:

['Joey', 'Chandler', 'Ross', 'Phoebe', 'Rachel', 'Geller']

It is that easy! You can use lists with loops and conditional statements to iterate over random elements and use the ones which are most suitable for the situation. Practice a little, and you should soon get the hang of them.

What about if we want to add numbers or values to the existing lists? Do we have to scroll all the way up and continue adding numbers manually? No! There are things called methods, which you can access at any given time to carry out various operations.

Here's a screenshot to show just how many options you have available to you once you enter the "." Symbol.

```
numbers = [99, 123, 2313, 1, 1231411, 343, 435345]
numbers.|
    insert(self, index, object)                          list
    append(self, object)                                 list
    clear(self)                                          list
    copy(self)                                           list
    count(self, object)                                  list
    extend(self, iterable)                               list
    index(self, object, start, stop)                     list
    pop(self, index)                                     list
    remove(self, object)                                 list
    reverse(self)                                        list
    sort(self, key, reverse)                             list
Ctrl+Down and Ctrl+Up will move caret down and up in the editor. Next Tip
```

We will not be talking about all of these, but we will briefly look at some basic methods that every programmer should know.

Straight away, the "append" method is what we use to add values. Simply type in the name of the list you wish to recall, followed by ".append" to let the program know that you want to add a value. Type in the value and that is it!

The problem with using the "append" method is that it adds the item randomly. What if you wish to add a value to a specific index number? To do that, you will need to use the "insert" method.

Using an "insert" method, you will need to do this:

numbers = [99, 123, 2313, 1, 1231411, 343, 435345]

numbers.insert(2, 999)

print(numbers)

Program Output:

[99, 123, 999, 2313, 1, 1231411, 343, 435345]

The number was added right where I wanted. Remember to use a valid index position. If you are unsure, use the "len()" function to recall how many components are within a list. That should then allow you to know the index positions available.

You can also remove items from a list as well. Simply use the "remove()" method and input the number/value you want to remove. Please note that if your list has values that are exactly the same, this command will only remove the first instance only.

Let us assume you are presented with a list of mixed entries; there is no order that they follow; the numbers are just everywhere, disregarding the order. If you want, you can sort the entire list to look more appealing by using the "sort()" method.

numbers = [99, 123, 2313, 1, 1231411, 99, 435345]

numbers.sort()

print(numbers)

Program Output:

[1, 99, 99, 123, 2313, 435345, 1231411]

Also, you can also have it the other way around by using the "reverse()" method. Try it!

To completely empty a list, you can use the "clear()" method. This specific method will not require you to pass any argument as a parameter. There are other methods such as "pop()"—it only takes away the last item on the list—that you should experiment with. Do not worry; it will not crash your system down or expose it to threats. Python IDE is like a safe zone for programmers to test out various methods, programs, and scripts. Feel free and feel at ease when charting new waters.

Tuples

As funny as the name may be, tuples are pretty much like lists. The only major difference is that these are used when you do not want certain specialized values to change throughout the program. Once you create a tuple, it cannot be modified or changed later on.

Tuples are represented by parenthesis (). If you try and access the methods, you will no longer have access to the methods that you did when you were using lists. These are secure and used only in situations where you are certain you do not want to change, modify, add, or remove items. Normally, we will be using lists, but it is great to know we have a safe way to do things as well.

Dictionaries

Unlike tuples and lists, dictionaries are different. To begin with, they work with "key-value pairs," which sounds confusing, I know. However, let us look at what exactly a dictionary is and how we can call, create, and modify the names.

To help us with the explanation, we have our imaginary friend here named "James," who has graciously accepted to volunteer for the exercise. We then take some information from him, such as his name, email, age, and the car he drives, and then we end up with this information:

Name – James

Age – 58

Email – james@domain.com

Car – Tesla T1

What we have here are called key-value pairs. To represent the same within a dictionary, all we need is to create one. How do we do that? Let's have a look:

friend = {

"name": "James",

"age": 30,

"email": "james@domain.com",

"car": "Tesla T1"

}

We define a dictionary using "{}." Add each key-value pair as shown above with a colon in the middle. Use a comma to separate items from one another. Now, you have a dictionary called "friend," and you can access the information easily.

Now, to call up the email, we will use square brackets as shown here:

friend = {

"name": "James",

"age": 30,

"email": "james@domain.com",

"car": "Tesla T1"

}

print(friend["email"])

Program Output:

james@domain.com

Unlike tuples, you can add, modify, or change values within a dictionary. I have already shown you how to do that with lists, but just for demonstration purposes, here's one way you can do that:

```
friend["age"] = 60

print(friend["age"])
```

Program Output:

```
60
```

Chapter 6: Numbers and Operators

Along with strings, numeric types, there are operators, which are important building blocks in coding. They help us count objects, perform math operations, keep track of things, and so much more. Don't worry, you can do this. Let's get started!

Numeric Types

There are two main numeric types that we'll be using in Python: Integers and floats. Integers are the whole numbers (positive or negative) that we are all used to. Floating-point numbers, or simply floats, are numbers that can have whole and fractional parts and are written using decimal points.

Operators

In programming, "operators" are special symbols or keywords that represent an action. They are usually used with "operands," which are the values you are performing the action on. In this section, our operands will be numbers. If you've ever used a calculator, then you should be familiar with a set of operators that are specifically used for math. These are called arithmetic operators.

Arithmetic Operators

Also known as the math operators, arithmetic operators are used to perform the basic math functions. As you'll see in the following chart, most arithmetic operators work just like they do in regular mathematics, with a few exceptions:

Operator Symbol	Operator Name	Action Taken	Example	Resulting Output
+	Addition	Adds values together.	4 + 5	9
-	Subtraction	Subtracts one value from another.	10 - 5 5 - 10	5 -5
*	Multiplication	Multiplies values together.	9 * 6	54
/	Division	Divides one value by another (answer will always be a float type).	8 / 4 9 / 4	2.0 2.25

%	Modulus	Divides one value by another, and the remainder is returned.	12 % 5 12 % 6	2 0
//	Floor Division	Divides one value by another, returns the answer rounded to the next smallest whole number.	4 // 3 4 // 2	1 2
**	Exponentiation	Raises one value to the power of another.	2 ** 5	32

To see these operations in action, go ahead and set the following variables in "Python shell":

a = 6

b = 3

Now you can begin using different operators on these variables directly in Python shell. Try out a few, like these:

a + b

b ** a

a % b

Cool, right? Now, to really get comfortable with them, try out all of the combinations and see what happens! You can check the answers on the following chart, although I think the computer is pretty good at math ;)…

Here are all the possible answers that can occur using the different operators and the variables:

Operator Combination	Answer	Operator Combination	Answer
a + b	9	a + a	12
b + a	9	a - a	0
a – b	3	a * a	36
b – a	-3	a / a	1.0
a * b	18	a % a	0

b * a	18	a // a	1
a / b	2.0	a ** a	46656
b / a	0.5	b + b	6
a % b	0	b - b	0
b % a	3	b * b	9
a // b	2	b / b	1.0
b // a	0	b % b	0
a ** b	216	b // b	1
b ** a	729	b ** b	27

Order of Operations

Arithmetic operators follow a special set of rules. This set of rules is called the order of operations. It is the proper order in which arithmetic operations should be calculated, especially if you use more than one in a single line of code.

Let's follow the order of operations—here's how:

Parentheses: In calculations like this, the computer always calculates any expression in parentheses first. Parentheses tell us 'I'm most important' in the rules of precedence in math.

Exponentiation: The next calculation that is performed is exponentiation. When the computer sees the "**" operator, it raises one number to the power of another.

Multiplication and Division: Multiplication and division have the same level of importance as each other, so if both a multiplication and division calculation appear in the same line, we start with the calculation on the left and work our way to the right.

Addition and Subtraction: The calculations with the least importance are addition and subtraction. This means they are performed last. Since addition and subtraction have the same level of importance, we use the left-to-right order of calculating them, just like we did with multiplication and division.

Comparison Operators

The next set of operators we use in programming are called comparison operators. Just like their name, comparison operators help us compare one value to another. When we use comparison operators, they give us back a "true" or "false" answer known as a "Boolean" type. Comparison operators and Booleans are super important because they help us make decisions in our code.

There are six main comparison operators, and they are pretty simple to understand. Let's talk about each one:

Greater than

The symbol ">" represents the greater-than operator.

When you use it, the computer decides whether the value on the left side of the > symbol is larger than the value on the right side of the > symbol.

Less than

The symbol ">=" represents the less-than operator.

This time, we are figuring out if the value on the left of the "<" symbol is less, or smaller than the value on the right side of the "<" symbol.

Greater than or Equal to

The symbol ">=" represents the greater-than-or-equal-to operator.

We're already familiar with the first symbol, so let's talk about the second symbol. We've used the equal sign (=) before to assign pieces of data to variables ("remember mood = happy"?). When we use it as an operator, though, we are partly deciding if the value on the left of the ">=" operator is equal to the value on the right of the ">=" operator.

But this operator is special since there are two symbols this time. We are trying to decide if the value on the left of the ">=" operator is greater than the one on the right, or if the value on the left is the same as the value on the right. Only one of these cases needs to be true for the computer to decide that the entire expression is "true."

Less than or Equal to

The symbol "<=" represents the less-than operator.

Just like the greater-than-or-equal-to operator, we are making sure at least one of the operators is correct. For the less-than-or-equal-to operator, we are looking at the values to see if the value on the left of the "<=" operator is either smaller than the one on the right of the "<=" operator or the same as the one on the right.

Equal to

The symbol "==" represents the equal-to operator.

This one is much simpler than the last two operators. Just like it sounds, it asks the computer to decide if the value on the left side of the "==" symbol is the same as the value on the right side of the "==" symbol. Easy!

The computer doesn't see integer and string types as the same types, either. So when we use the equal-to operator, remember that the computer will check that the values are the same type and the same value/number/text.

Not Equal to

Last one! You're so awesome for making it this far! The symbol "!=" represents the not-equal-to operator.

Also, like the name, the not-equal-to operator asks the computer to figure out if the value on the left side of the "!=" symbol is not the same as the value on the right side of the "!=" symbol.

Logical Operators

Logical operators are used to help us compare true or false operands. These are very helpful because they can make our decision-making rules more complex, which means smarter code! There are three main logical operators: "And," "or," and "not." Let's see what each can do.

And

The "and" operator checks that the values on the right and left of it are both "True."

If there's a point in our code that should only run when two conditions are met, we should use the "and" operator. Imagine that you're going through a pizza buffet and you need to pick only the slices of pizza that you like. You like pepperoni and you like mushrooms, and you'd love to pick up a slice or two of that kind of pizza if it had both of those toppings.

While walking around, you sadly see that there's only a pizza with pepperoni but no mushrooms. Let's say we had variables that held this information:

pizza_has_pepperoni = True

pizza_has_mushrooms = False

To check that the pizza you were evaluating had both pepperoni and mushrooms, you'd use the "and" operator like this:

pizza_has_pepperoni and pizza_has_mushrooms True

The "and" operator allows you to check both conditions—that the pizza slice has pepperoni and that it has mushrooms. Only then would you take a slice of pizza, if both conditions were met! Unfortunately, you won't be taking a slice, since only one condition is "True" :(...

Or

The "or" operator makes sure that at least one value being compared is "True."

Going back to our pizza example, let's say that you couldn't find any pizza that had both pepperoni and mushroom on it (bummer). Still wanting pizza, you decide that if the pizza has either pepperoni or mushroom on it, you'll select that pizza. Here is where the "or" operator will come in handy. To check for either pepperoni or mushroom, you'd write code like this:

```
pizza_has_pepperoni or pizza_has_mushrooms
```

That way, if the pizza you were checking had either pepperoni or mushroom on it, you'd take it.

Not

The "not" operator checks to make sure that the value being compared is "False."

Just as you'd take any pizza that had pepperoni or mushroom on it, you would definitely not take any that had onions on it. Let's say we had a variable called "pizza_has_onions" and its value was "True." To make sure you don't get any pizza with onions on it, you could use the "not" operator:

```
not pizza_has_onion
```

It looks a little funny if you try to read it out loud, but it is correct! You're basically saying, "Hey, computer, make sure that the fact of the pizza having onions is not true."

Chapter 7: Operators in Python

There is a variety of functions available in Python to work with numbers. Let's look at a summary of them, after which we will look at each in more detail along with a simple example for each.

Function	Description
abs()	This returns the absolute value of a number.
ceil()	This returns the ceiling value of a number.
max()	This returns the largest value in a set of numbers.
min()	This returns the smallest value in a set of numbers.
pow(x,y)	This returns the power of x to y.
sqrt()	This returns the square root of a number.

random()	This returns a random value.
randrange(start,stop,step)	This returns a random value from a particular range.
sin(x)	This returns the sin value of a number.
cos(x)	This returns the cosine value of a number.
tan(x)	This returns the tangent value of a number.

Abs Function

This function returns the absolute value of a number.

Example: The following program shows the "abs" function.

```
# This program looks at number functions

a=-1.23

print(abs(a))
```

This program's output will be as follows:

Ceil Function

This function is used to return the ceiling value of a number. Note that for this program, we need to import the "math" module in order to use the "ceil" function.

Example: The following program shows the ceil function:

```
import math

# This program looks at number functions

a=1.23

print(math.ceil(a))
```

This program's output will be as follows:

2

Max Function

This function returns the largest value in a set of numbers.

Example: The program below is used to show the "max" function.

```
# This program looks at number functions
```

```
print(max(3,4,5))
```

This program's output will be as follows:

5

Min Function

This function returns the smallest value in a set of numbers.

Example: The following program shows how the "min" function works.

```
# This program looks at number functions

print(min(3,4,5))
```

This program's output will be as follows:

3

Pow Function

This function returns the value of "x" to the power of "y," where the syntax is "pow(x,y)."

Example: The following program shows the "pow" function:

```
# This program looks at number functions
```

```
print(pow(2,3))
```

This program's output will be as follows:

8

Sqrt Function

This function returns the square root of a number. Note that for this program, we need to import the "math" module to use the "sqrt" function.

Example: The next program shows how the "sqrt" function works:

```
import math

# This program looks at number functions

print(math.sqrt(9))
```

This program's output will be as follows:

3

Random Function

This function is used to return a random value.

Example: The following program shows the random function:

```
import random

# This program looks at number functions

print(random.random())
```

The output will differ depending on the random number generated. Also, note that for this program, we need to use the "random" Python library. In our case, the program's output is:

0.005460085356885691

Randrange Function

This function is used to return a random value from a particular range. Note that we again need to import the "random" library for this function to work.

Example: This program is used to show the random function:

```
import random

# This program looks at number functions

print(random.randrange(1,10,2))
```

The output will differ depending on the random number generated. In our case, the program's output is:

5

Sin Function

This function returns the sine value of a number.

Example: The following program shows how to use the sin function:

```
import math

# This program looks at number functions

print(math.sin(45))
```

This program's output will be as follows:

0.8509035245341184

Cos Function

This function returns the cosine value of a number.

Example: This program is used to showcase the "cos" function:

```
import math

# This program looks at number functions
```

```
print(math.cos(45))
```

This program's output will be as follows:

0.5253219888177297

Tan Function

This function returns the tangent value of a number.

Example: The following program shows the use of the "tan" function:

```
import math

# This program looks at number functions

print(math.tan(45))
```

This program's output will be as follows:

1.6197751905438615

DAY 3: Developing Code

Chapter 8: Installation and Running of Python

It is simple to install and run Python on all operating systems, but considering the scope of this book, I will show you how to go about that on "Windows."

Unlike other operating systems, it is very unlikely that your Windows OS came with Python already installed. The good thing is that installing Python does not involve anything more than downloading the installer and running it. Just take the following steps:

Download the Installer

Open your browser and go to "Python.org" on the "download page for Windows."

You will see "Python releases for Windows" as shown below. Click on the **latest Python 3 release – 3.7.1.**

Python »» Downloads »» Windows

Python Releases for Windows

- Latest Python 3 Release - Python 3.7.1
- Latest Python 2 Release - Python 2.7.15

- Python 3.7.1 - 2018-10-20

Now scroll to the bottom and choose "Windows x86-64 executable installer" to get the Windows x86 or 64-bit executable installer as shown in the image below:

macOS 64-bit/32-bit installer	Mac OS X
macOS 64-bit installer	Mac OS X
Windows help file	Windows
Windows x86-64 embeddable zip file	Windows
Windows x86-64 executable installer	Windows
Windows x86-64 web-based installer	Windows
Windows x86 embeddable zip file	Windows
Windows x86 executable installer	Windows
Windows x86 web-based installer	Windows

The Difference between the 32-Bit and 64-Bit Python

You can select the 64-bit installer or the 32-bit installer when it comes to Windows and what determines your choice is your system's processor.

If your computer is running on a 32-bit processor, you can select the 32-bit installer.

If your PC is running on a 64-bit processor, either installer will be able to work for most purposes. The 32-bit version generally uses less memory; the 64-bit version on the other hand performs better for applications with high computation.

If you are not sure which version to select, just pick the 64-bit version.

Once you click the appropriate link, a file labeled "Python-3.7.1-amd64.exe" will start downloading to your computer—it is about 25 MB. You can move the file to a more permanent area in your computer so that you install the program, and if necessary, reinstall it more easily later.

Run Your Installer

Having selected and downloaded your installer, you can now double click on the downloaded file to have a dialog box pop up.

Note: Don't forget to check the box that reads "add Python 3.x to PATH" to make sure the "interpreter" (a computer program that translates instructions in a program written in a high-level computer language into machine language and executes them) is positioned in your execution path.

Finish by clicking on **Install Now** to complete the installation.

Starting the Interpreter

Once the installation is complete, the Python interpreter resides in the installed directory.

By default, it is:

C:\pythonxx in widows and /usr/local/bin/python x.x

Here, 'x' stands for the version number. Invoking it from the command prompt or shell will require you to enter the location in the search path.

A search path is a list of locations or directories where the OS looks for an executable. For instance, you can type the text in the image below in "Windows Command Prompt" to have the location added to the path for that session in particular.

"set path=%path%;c:\python37"

Note: "Python37" means version 3.7; your case might be different

For "Mac OS," you don't have to worry about this because the installer will take care of the path.

Start the Python

Type "Python" in the command line to power up the interpreter in "immediate" mode. You can key in Python expressions directly and hit "Enter" to obtain the output.

Note: ">>>" represents the output prompt, which informs you that the interpreter is prepared to take your input. When you type in "2 + 2" and tap "Enter," you will receive "4" as the output. You can use this prompt as a calculator. If you want to leave this mode, just type "quit()" or "exit()" and tap "Enter."

Integrated Development Environment (IDE)

You can write a Python script file or instructions with any text editor; all you have to do is save it with the extension ".py." However, if you want to make your life much easier, you can use an IDE. An IDE is a software that offers you, the programmer, important features such as syntax highlighting and checking, code hinting, file explorers, and so on.

By using an IDE, you remove redundant tasks and reduce the time you need for actual programming.

Python comes with its own environment—known as "Python IDLE" (integrated development and learning environment)—that serves this purpose. You can use it to write, edit, debug (remove errors), and run Python programs. When you install a modern Python version on your computer, IDLE is automatically installed along with it. You can therefore access IDLE through the "Start" menu on a Windows computer. If you are using Linux or Mac that has Python installed on it, simply type "idle" at the command line.

Congratulations! You can now write your first program!

Chapter 9: Execution and Statement about a Program

So far, you have learned the basics about Python programs. Now it's time to learn how to enter programs into the computer, execute them, see how they perform and see how they display the results.

An integrated development environment (IDE) is a type of software that enables programmers to both write and execute their source code. "Python IDLE" and "Eclipse" are such examples.

Creating a New Python Module

Once you open IDLE, the first thing you see is the "Python Shell" window, as shown in the image below:

```
Python 3.6.0 Shell                                    —    □    ×
File  Edit  Shell  Debug  Options  Window  Help
Python 3.6.0 (v3.6.0:41df79263a11, Dec 23 2016, 07:18:10) [MSC v
.1900 32 bit (Intel)] on win32
Type "copyright", "credits" or "license()" for more information.
>>> |




                                                          Ln: 3  Col: 4
```

Python Shell is an environment where you can type statements that are immediately executed. For example, if you type "7 + 3 "and hit the "Enter" key, the Python Shell will directly display the result of this operation.

However, you should not write a Python program within the Python Shell window. To write a Python program, create a new Python file (known as a Python module). From Python Shell's main menu select "File - New File" as shown in the following image:

In the image below you can see the new empty module where you will write your Python programs!

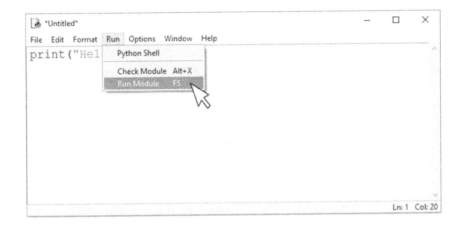

Writing and Executing a Python Program

You have just seen how to create a new Python module. In the recently created window "Untitled", type the following (terrifying, and quite horrifying) Python program.

Print ("Hello World")

Now let's try to execute the program! From the main menu, select "Run - Run Module" as shown in the image below, or hit the "F5" key.

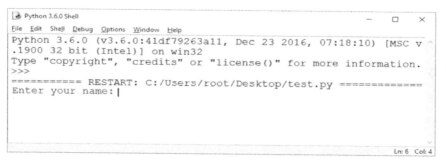

```
Python 3.6.0 Shell                                          —    □    ×
File  Edit  Shell  Debug  Options  Window  Help
Python 3.6.0 (v3.6.0:41df79263a11, Dec 23 2016, 07:18:10) [MSC v
.1900 32 bit (Intel)] on win32
Type "copyright", "credits" or "license()" for more information.
>>>
=========== RESTART: C:/Users/root/Desktop/test.py ============
Hello World
>>> |

                                                          Ln: 6  Col: 4
```

Executing your first Python program!

The Python IDLE prompts you to save the source code. Click on the **OK** button, select a folder and filename for your first program, and click on the **Save** button. The Python program is saved and executed, and then the output is displayed in the Python Shell window, as shown below:

```
Python 3.6.0 Shell                                          —    □    ×
File  Edit  Shell  Debug  Options  Window  Help
Python 3.6.0 (v3.6.0:41df79263a11, Dec 23 2016, 07:18:10) [MSC v
.1900 32 bit (Intel)] on win32
Type "copyright", "credits" or "license()" for more information.
>>>
=========== RESTART: C:/Users/root/Desktop/test.py ============
Enter your name: |

                                                          Ln: 6  Col: 4
```

Viewing the results of the executed program in the Python Shell window.

Congratulations! You have just written and executed your first Python program!

Now let's write another Python program, one that prompts the user to enter his or her name. Type the following Python program and hit "F5" to execute the file.

file_ 7_3

Name = input ("Enter your name: ")

Print ("Hello" , name)

Print ("Have a nice day!")

Once you execute the program, the message "Enter your name:" is displayed in the Python Shell window without the double quotes. The program waits for you to enter your name, as shown in the following image:

```
Python 3.6.0 Shell                                    —  □  ×
File  Edit  Shell  Debug  Options  Window  Help
Python 3.6.0 (v3.6.0:41df79263a11, Dec 23 2016, 07:18:10) [MSC v
.1900 32 bit (Intel)] on win32
Type "copyright", "credits" or "license()" for more information.
>>>
============ RESTART: C:/Users/root/Desktop/test.py =============
Enter your name: Zeus
Hello Zeus
Have a nice day!
>>> |
                                                        Ln: 6  Col: 4
```

Viewing a prompt in the Python Shell window.

Type your name and hit the "Enter" key. Once you do that, your computer continues to execute the rest of the statements. When the execution finishes, the final output is as shown in the image:

```
Python 3.6.0 Shell                                            —    □    ×
File  Edit  Shell  Debug  Options  Window  Help
Python 3.6.0 (v3.6.0:41df79263a11, Dec 23 2016, 07:18:10) [MSC v
.1900 32 bit (Intel)] on win32
Type "copyright", "credits" or "license()" for more information.
>>>
=========== RESTART: C:/Users/root/Desktop/test.py ============
Enter number A: 5
Enter number B: 0
Traceback (most recent call last):
  File "C:/Users/root/Desktop/test.py", line 3, in <module>
    c = num1 / num2
ZeroDivisionError: float division by zero
>>> |
                                                            Ln: 6  Col: 4
```

Responding to the prompt in the Python Shell window.

Chapter 10: Python Modules

Working with Modules in Python

"Python modules" empower you to part portions of your program in various documents for simpler support and better performance.

As a fledgling, you begin working with Python on the interpreter; later, when you have to write longer programs, you begin writing scripts. As your program develops more in size, you might need to part it into a few records for simpler support as well as reusability of the code. The answer to this is "Python modules." You can characterize your most utilized capacities in a module and import it somewhere else, rather than duplicating their definitions into various projects. A module can be brought in by an additional program to utilize its functionality—you can also use the Python standard library this way.

A module is a file consisting of Python code. It can define functions, classes, and factors; furthermore, it can likewise incorporate runnable code. Any Python record can be referenced as a module. A document containing Python code, for instance, "test.py," is known as a module, and its name would be tested.

There are different strategies for writing modules. However, the least complex path is to make a ".py" document that contains these capacities and factors.

Instructional exercises will help you through writing your Python modules. You will find out about the following topics:

- The import statement in Python

- Writing modules

- More on import statements

- Module search path

- Byte compiled files

- The "dir()" function

The Import Statement

To utilize the capabilities of any module, you need to bring it into your current program. You have to utilize the "import" keyword along with the ideal module name. When the "translator" (a computer program that converts other programs from one computer language into another) runs over an import command, it imports the module to your present program. You can utilize the functions in a module by utilizing a "speck(.)" operator along with the module name. To initiate, how about we observe how to utilize the standard library modules. In the model below, the math module is brought into the program to use the "sqrt()" function defined in it.

For efficiency reasons, every module is just imported once per interpreter session. Thus, if you change your modules, you should restart the interpreter; if it's only one module, you need to test interactively, use "reload()"; for instance, "reload(module_name)."

Writing Modules

Since you have figured out how to import a module in your program, the time has come to write your own, and use it in another program. Writing a module is much the same as writing some other Python file. We should begin by writing a function to add/subtract two numbers in a record calculation.

```
def add(x,y):
    return (x+y)
def sub(x,y):
    return (x-y)
```

In case you attempt to execute the code in the image above, nothing will happen because you have not taught the program to do anything. Make another python script in a similar index with the name "module_test.py," and write the following code into it:

```
import calculation        #Importing calculation module
print(calculation.add(1,2))   #Calling function defined in add module.
```

When the translator went over the import statement, it imported the calculation module in your code, and afterwards by utilizing the "dot" operator, you had the option to get to the "include()" function.

More on Import Statements

There are more approaches to import the modules:

- From…import statement
- From…import* statement
- Retitling the imported module

From…Import Statement

The "from…import" statement permits you to import explicit functions/variables from a module as opposed to bringing in all things. In the past model, when you brought "count" into "module_test.py," both the "add()" and "sub()" capacities were imported. Nevertheless, envision a situation where you just require the "add()" function in your code.

Here is a guide to representing the utilization of "from…import":

from calculation import add

the print(add(1,2))

In the above model, just the "add()" function is imported and utilized. Notice the utilization of include()? You would now be able to get to it directly without utilizing the module name. You can import various qualities too, isolating them by separating with a comma in the import statement. Study the following model:

from count import add, sub

From…Import* Statement

You can import all characteristics of a module using this statement. This will make all characteristics of the imported module noticeable in your code.

However, here is a guide to representing the utilization of "from .. import *":

```
from calculation import *
print(add(1,2))
print(sub(3,2))
```

Note that in the expert world, you ought to avoid utilizing "from…import" and "from…import*," as doing so makes your code less readable.

Renaming the Imported Module

You can rename the module you are importing, which can be helpful in situations when you need to give a more meaningful name to the module, or when the module name is too vast even to consider using it more than once. You can utilize it as a keyword to rename it. The following example explains how to utilize it in your program.

```
import calculation as cal
print(cal.add(1,2))
```

You save yourself some code writing time by renaming calculation as cal.

Note that you presently can't utilize calculation any longer, as the calculation is not, at this point recognized in your program, so use "add (1,2)."

Module Search Path

You may require your modules to be utilized in various projects/programs, and their physical area in the directory can be different. If you need to utilize a module from some other catalog, you have a few options provided by Python.

When you import a module named calculation, the interpreter first searches for an implicit module with that name. If not discovered, then it scans for a document named "calculation.py" in a rundown of registries given by the variable "sys.path."

"sys.path" contains these areas:

- The catalog contains the input script (or the current registry).
- Python path (a list of directory names, with a similar syntax to the shell variable "path").
- The installation-dependent default.

The access to the "module_test.py" is in the "/home/datacamp" catalog, and you moved "calculation.py" to "/home/test/." You can alter "sys.path" to incorporate "/home/test/" in the list of ways, wherein the Python interpreter will search for the module. For this, you have to alter "module_test.py" in the following way:

```
import sys
sys.path.append('/home/test/')

import calculation
print(calculation.add(1,2))
```

Byte-Compiled Files

Importing a module builds the execution time of projects, so Python has a few stunts to speed it up. One route is to create byte-compiled files with the ".pyc" extension.

Inside, Python changes over the source code into an intermediate form called "byte code"; it then interprets this into the native language of your PC and then runs it. This ".pyc" record is helpful whenever you import the module from a different program—it will be a lot faster since a bit of the processing required for importing a module is already done. Additionally, these byte-compiled files are platform-independent.

Note that these ".pyc" files are normally made in a similar index as the comparing ".py" files. If Python doesn't have permission to write documents in that registry, then the ".pyc" files won't be made.

The dir() function

The "dir()" function is utilized to discover all the names characterized in a module. It restores a sorted list of strings containing the names defined in a module.

```
import calculation
print(test.add(1,2))
print(dir(calculation))
```

Output:
['__builtins__','__cached__','__doc__','__file__','__loader__','__name__','__package__','__spec__', 'add', 'sub']

In the image, you can see the names of the capacities you characterized in the module, including "sub." The characteristic "__name__" contains the name of the module. All traits starting with an underscore are default python attributes related to a module.

Chapter 11: Classes and Objects

So far, we've seen that Python largely depends on the organization and collection of data from lists, which are a collection of variables, and functions, which are a collection of collecting codes together, so you can call or recall them whenever you need them. Modules also stem from functions, as a collection of these functions. There's another form of classification referred to as "objects." Being able to collect functions and variables (data) together is the reason why objects exist. It's yet an easier way to classify your codes into smaller things, which eventually build up into a complex idea.

To understand this better, here's a simple illustration. If you're asked to think up two random things, you'll come up with the most random things, but we'll use book and puppy for now. Go a further step by trying to think about these two objects. What are they? Describe them as much as you can. For the puppy, you'll probably use terms like, "animal," "living thing," "smaller dog," etc. For the book, you'll probably say that it's an inanimate object, and the color it has.

Using the terms "animal," "animate objects," "smaller dog," is the way of classifying the things you've listed.

You may hear programmers say, "Python is object-oriented." The objects they refer to here are the collection of codes and variables together. The fun thing about objects is that they're quite easy to use, and although you can, you don't as a matter of necessity have to create them yourself. We'll now go ahead to learn how to create and use them.

Objects in Python

Random things such as books are regarded as "objects." The things you know about these things like size, color, etc. are the attributes (and are usually in variables). The things you can do with these objects are referred to as the methods. For you to easily remember:

- Thing = object
- Features of thing = attribute
- Things you can do with the thing = methods

Using our first example – book –,

- Book = object
- Color, size, weight, number of pages = attributes
- Read, write, open = methods

Now let's see how these will look in a Python interactive shell:

book.color

book.size

book.weight

book.page_number

book.read()

book.write()

book.flip()

When displaying the attributes:

print book.color

When assigning values to them:

book.color = black

When assigning them to regular, nonobject variables:

myColor = book.color

When assigning them to attributes in other objects:

myBook.color = yourBook.color

Objects are essentially made up of attributes and methods. You're collecting the things you know about the things and what they can do together in one place.

This may just be the perfect time to explain what the dot "(.)" is representing in the codes you've been writing. It's referred to as the dot notation, and it's needed when you want to use the attributes and methods of the objects. We may now go ahead to learn to create this object.

Creating Objects in Python

There're two things to be done when creating objects.

First off, you need to describe how the object will look like and act like. It's like putting together the blueprint for a project. This blueprint makes you understand the features of the thing you're trying to build (attributes), and how they can work (methods), even before they are created. That's exactly how it works in programming. The blueprint you create for your object is referred to as the "class." Once the class has been created, then you move on to the next step.

Creating the object with its blueprint ("class") is the next step. If you think about it, that's how things in life work. You want to build a house, you put up a blueprint first. Then you use the blueprint to build the actual house. It helps you understand how to go about the building and reaching your goal. You're creating an "object" at the instance of that "class." If we want to create a class for our example above, here's how it'll look:

```
class Book:

def flip(self):

if self.direction == 'left':

self.direction = 'right'
```

Here, we've defined the book with the method "flip()." Attributes, however, can't be created this way because they don't really belong in a class, but to each instance. All attributes will belong to different instances.

Creating an Instance of an Object

Since we already have a class now, we'll go ahead to create an instance of an object from it. For the instance of "Book," we do it this way:

myBook = Book()

Our book has no attributes yet, so we'll give it some:

myBook.direction = "right"

myBook.direction = "left"

myBook.color = "black"

myBook.size = "large"

There's another way of defining attributes in an object, but we'll be exploring that as we go on.

Now that we've defined attributes, we can go ahead to try out some of the methods. Let's use the "flip()" method:

myBook.flip()

You can go ahead to input it in the Python interactive shell and print them to see the outcome.

```
class Book:

def flip(self):

if self.direction == 'left':

self.direction = 'right'

myBook= Book()

myBook.direction = "right"

myBook.direction = "left"

myBook.color = "black"

myBook.size = "large"

print("I just bought a book.")

print("My book is", myBook.size)

print("My book is", myBook.color)

print("My book flips to the", myBook.direction)

print("Now I'll flip the book again")

print

myBook.flips()

print "Now the book's flipped to the", myBook.direction
```
108

The code above should give you:

I just bought a book.

My book is large

My book is black

My book flips to the left

Now I'm going to flip the book again

Now the book's flipped to the right

The "flip()" method, when called the first time, flips the book to the left and later changes the direction from left to right. That is exactly what the code in the "flip()" method was created to do.

Python 'Magic' Methods

Initializing an Object (_init_ method)

There's a special method that can be used to run the code whenever you create a new instance of the class you have defined. This method is called "_init_()," and it creates the instance with the properties set whichever way you want. Here's how to go about it:

class Book:

def _init_ (self, color, size, direction):

```
self.color = color

self.size = size

self.direction = direction

def flip(self):

if self.direction == 'left':

self.direction = 'right'

myBook= Book("black", "large", "left")

print("I just bought a book.")

print("My book is", myBook.size)

print("My book is", myBook.color)

print("My book flips to the", myBook.direction)

print("Now I'll flip the book again")

print

myBook.flips()

print "Now the book's flipped to the", myBook.direction
```

If done correctly, you'll get the same output as the last code. The only difference is that you use the "_init_" method to run the instances defined in your object class.

The _str_ Method

This method tells Python what to show when you print an object. There's an existing "_str_" method in all Python objects. If you don't create yours, the already existing one is what Python is going to use by default in printing your object. But if you want to display something else with your print function, you can define your own "_str_" to override the default one. In the simplest terms, this method changes how the object prints. Let's see an example.

class Book:

def __init__(self, color, size, direction):

self.color = color

self.size = size

self.direction = direction

def __str__(self):

msg = "Check out my new book. It is " + self.size + " " + self.color"

return msg

myBook = Book("black", "large", "left")

```
print myBook
```

After running your program, you should get:

Check out my new book. It is large and black

Hiding Data

There are two ways through which you can change or view the attributes inside an object. You can either access an attribute directly by:

"myPiece.finish_level = 6"

Or:

"myPiece.paint(5)."

The second method of modifying the attribute is usually used because the first allows for decreasing of the "finish_level." Accessing the attribute means that you're changing at least two parts (the "finish_level" and the "finish_string"). Thus, we need a method that makes sure the "finish_level" doesn't reduce but only increases.

Data hiding is the restriction of access to an object's variable so you can just use it or change it by using methods. Python doesn't have a means of enforcing this data hiding, you can just write code that follows this rule if you want to.

There's just one more aspect of classes and objects that you need to learn, and they're polymorphism and inheritance. You may have an idea what

112

inheritance is, but there's a 90% chance you've never heard of polymorphism—same method, same name, but different behavior.

Polymorphism means having two or even more methods that have the same name but are in different classes. As much as you may try not to, it's not impossible that this happens. You may get to use polymorphism a lot when calculating mathematics, especially in geometry. Here's an example:

```python
class Square:

    def __init__(self, size):

        self.size = size

    def findArea(self):

        area = self.size * self.size

        return area

class Triangle:

    def __init__(self, breadth, height):

        self.breadth = breadth

        self.height = height

    def findArea(self):

        area = self.breath * self.height / 2.0
```

```
    return area
```

That's the formula for getting the areas of a square and triangle respectively. There's the method "findArea" in both classes. But they behave differently. When you add the print statement, you'll be able to calculate the areas differently. First, call the instance of each class.

```
>>> mySquare = Square(12)

>>> myTriangle = Triangle(8, 10)

>>> mySquare.getArea()

144

>>> myTriangle.getArea()

40.0
```

Tips 'N' Tricks

- Class names usually start with block letters (like we used in the class "Book"). It's not a rule, but it's just a convention that makes things easier for you and your code—long live the programming tradition.
- Codes are getting even longer. But you must type them all into the Python shell. You'd never know what you know and don't unless you try!

- **The Hashtag (#):** You may have noticed in the last code we wrote in this chapter, that instead of inputting the codes we wanted the computer to process, we used a comment line to explain what should be inside, and started the line with a hashtag. Oftentimes when writing complex codes, programmers aren't always sure about what should be inside some functions yet. But they still have to write those codes. They employ this method. It's a way of thinking or planning ahead. These "empty" functions or methods (or whatever they may be in the code) are called code stubs. Although they aren't exactly empty, the comments written there don't add up to anything in Python language.

You may, or may not use the "pass" keyword while using code stubs. Using this keyword tells Python to ignore that code and jump to the next.

Chapter 12: Functions, Inputs, and Outputs

Functions

Functions are code blocks that are given an identifier. This identifier can be used to call the function. Calling a function makes the program execute the function regardless of where it is located within the code.

To create a function, you need to use the "def" keyword. When you use it to create a function, you can call it defining a function. For example:

```
>>> def doSomething():

    print("Hello functioning world!")

>>> doSomething()

Hello functioning world!

>>> _
```

Creating and calling a function is easy. The primary purpose of a function is to allow you to organize, simplify, and modularize your code. Whenever you have a set of code that you will need to execute in sequence from time to time, defining a function for that set of code will save you time and space in your program. Instead of repeatedly typing code or even copy-pasting, you simply define a function.

Return Statement

Return statements are useful when you wish to create functions whose sole job is to return some values.

Let us start by defining a function called "cube," which will basically multiply the number by itself three times. However, since we want Python to return a value, we will use the following code:

```
def cube(number):

return number * number * number
```

By typing "return" you are informing Python that you wish for it to return a value to you that can later be stored in a variable or used elsewhere. It is pretty much like the "input()" function where a user enters something and it gets returned to us.

```
def cube(number):

return number * number * number

number = int(input("Enter the number: "))

print(cube(number))
```

How to Define and Call Functions?

117

To start, we need to take a look at how we are able to define our own functions in this language. The function in Python is going to be defined when we use the statement of "def" and then follow it with a function name and some parentheses in place as well.

Some of the Python rules that we need to follow for defining these functions will include:

1. Any of the arguments or input parameters that you would like to use have to be placed within the parentheses so that the compiler knows what is going on.

2. The function first statement is something that can be an optional statement—something like a documentation string that goes with your function if needed.

3. The code found within all the functions that we are working with needs to start out with a colon, and then we need to indent it as well.

4. The "return" statement we get will need to exit a function at this time. We can then have the option of passing back a value to the caller. A return statement that doesn't have an argument with it is going to give us the same return as none.

Parameters

Parameters Require Arguments

You cannot call a function with parameters without an argument. If you do, you will receive an error. For example:

118

```
>>> def sampFunc(x):

    print(x)

>>> sampFunc()

Traceback (most recent call last):

  File "<stdin>", line 1, in <module>

TypeError: y() missing 1 required positional argument: 'x'

>>> _
```

Multiple Parameters

You can assign two or more parameters in a function. For example:

```
>>> def simpOp(x, y):

    z = x + y

    print(z)

>>> simpOp(1, 2)

3

>>> _
```

Return statement—Returning Value

The return keyword makes a function return a value. For a simpler explanation, it makes the function be used as a variable that has an assigned or processed value. For example:

```
>>> def concat(string1, string2):

      return string1 + string2

>>> x = concat("Text1", "Text2")

>>> x

'Text1Text2'

>>> _
```

A function can return a value even if it does not have parameters. For example:

```
>>> def piString():

      return "3.14159265359"

>>> x = piString()

>>> x

'3.14159265359'

>>> _
```

As you can see, using the keyword return makes it simpler for you to retrieve a value from a function without relying on global variables. Return allows you to write a clean and efficient code.

Lambda function—Anonymous Functions or Lambda

Using an anonymous function is a convenient way to write one-line functions that require arguments and return a value. The keyword "lambda" is an example of that. Despite having the purpose of writing one-line code, it can have numerous parameters. For example:

>>> average = lambda x, y, z: (x + y + z) / 3

>>> x = average(10, 20, 30)

>>> x

20.0

>>> average(12, 51, 231)

98.0

>>> _

Inputs

So far, we've only been writing programs that only use data we have explicitly defined in the script. However, your programs can also take in input from a user and utilize it. Python lets us solicit inputs from the user with a very intuitive function named "input()." Utilizing the "input()" function enables us to prompt the user to enter information, which we can further manipulate. For example, we can take the user's input and save it as a variable, print it straight to the terminal, or do anything else we might like.

When we use the input function, we can "pass" in a string. The user will see this string as a prompt, and their response to the prompt will be saved as the input value. For instance, if we wanted to query the user for their favorite food, we could write the following:

favorite_food = input("What is your favorite food?: ")

If you ran this code example, you would be prompted to input your favorite food. You could save multiple variables this way and print them all at once using the "print()" function along with print formatting, as we covered earlier. To be clear, the text you write in the input function is what the user will see as a prompt; it isn't what you are inputting into the system as a value.

When you run the code above, you'll be prompted for input. After you type in some text and hit the "Enter/Return" key, the text you wrote will be stored as the variable "favorite_food." The input command can be used along with string formatting to inject variables into the text prompt that the user will see. For instance, if we had a variable called "user_name" that stored the name of the user, we could structure the input statement like this:

```
favorite_food = input("What is {}'s favorite food?: ").format("user name here")
```

Printing and Formatting Outputs

We've already dealt with the "print()" function quite a bit, but let's take some time to address it again here and learn a bit more about its advanced features.

By now, you've gathered that it prints out whatever is in the parentheses of the function to the terminal. Besides, you've learned that you can format the printing of statements with either the modulus operator "%" or the format function ".format()." However, what should we do if we are in the process of printing a very long message?

In order to prevent a long string from running across the screen, we can use triple quotes to surround our string. Printing with triple quotes allows us to separate our print statements onto multiple lines. For example, we could print like this:

```
print('''By using triple quotes we can

divide our print statement into multiple

lines, making it easier to read.''')
```

Formatting the print statement like that will give us:

By using triple quotes we can

divide our print statement into multiple

lines, making it easier to read.

What if we need to print characters that are equivalent to string formatting instructions? For example, if we ever needed to print out the characters "%s" or "%d", we would run into trouble. If you recall, these are string formatting commands, and if we try to print these out, the interpreter will interpret them as formatting commands.

Here's a practical example. As mentioned, typing "/t" in our string will put a tab in the middle of our string. Assume we type the following:

print("We want a \t here, not a tab.")

We'd get back this:

We want a   here, not a tab.

By using an escape character, we can tell Python to include the characters that come next as part of the string's value. The escape character we want to use is the "raw string" character, an "r" before the first quote in a string, like this:

print(r"We want a \t here, not a tab.")

So, if we used the raw string character, we'd get the format we want back, as follows:

We want a \t here, not a tab.

The raw string character enables you to put any combination of characters you'd like within the string and have it be considered as part of the string's value.

However, what if we did want the tab in the middle of our string? In that case, using special formatting characters in our string is referred to as using "escape characters." "Escaping" a string is a method of reducing the ambiguity in how characters are interpreted. When we use an escape character, we escape the typical method that Python uses to interpret certain characters, and the characters we type are understood to be part of the string's value. The escape primarily used in Python is the backslash "\." The backslash prompts Python to look for a unique character to follow, which will be translated into a specific string formatting command.

We already saw that using the "\t" escape character puts a tab in the middle of our string, but there are other escape characters we can use as well, and they are shown below:

\n - Starts a new line

\\- Prints out a backslash itself

\" - Prints out a double quote instead of a double quote marking the end of a string

\' - Like above, but prints out a single quote

Chapter 13: Fun Projects and Games

Now that you've finished learning all the fundamentals of programming with Python, it's time to put everything together into practice.

Rock, Paper, Scissors

The first game will be "rock paper scissors," which is normally played by two people, but in this case, it's going to be you against the computer. When creating a game, the first thing we need to do is brainstorming. Take a pen and paper and think about how the game should be designed. Start out by first considering the rules of the game, and only then worry about the actual programming.

This classic game involves choosing one of three objects, as the name suggests. Once both selections are made, the items are revealed to see who wins. The player who wins is determined by three simple rules. The rock will crush the scissors, the scissors cut paper, and the paper covers the rock.

To handle these rules we are going to create a list of choices, similar to the list of colors we created before in some of our drawing programs. Then we will add a random selection function that will represent the choice the computer makes. Next, the human player will have to make his or her choice. Finally, the winner is decided with the help of some if statements.

Before we continue with the code, you should start performing these steps on your own. You already have the plan and you know which steps you need to take. So, simply break down the game into easy sections and work on one at a time. So give it a try before you read the following code.

Have you tried to create your own version of the game yet? If so, good job! Even if you didn't completely finish it, or you wrote the game and you're getting some errors, you should still reward yourself for trying. Now, let's go through the code and see how this game should turn out:

import random

selectionChoices = ["rock", "paper", "scissors"]

print ("Rock beats scissors. Scissors cut paper. Paper covers rock.")

```
player = input ("Do you want to choose rock, paper, or scissors? (or quit)
?"

while player != "quit":

    player = player.lower ()

computer   =   random.choice(selectionChoices)

print("You selected " +player+  ",

and the  computer  selected"  +computer+  ".")

if player == computer:

print("Draw!")

elif  player == "rock":

if computer == "scissors":

print ("Victory!")

else:

print("You lose!")

elif  player == "paper":

if computer == "rock":

print("Victory!")
```

```
else:

print(”You lose!”)

elif player == “scissors”:

if computer == “paper”:

print (”Victory!”) else:

print(”You lose!”)

else:

print(”Something went wrong…”)

print()

player = input (“Do you want to choose rock, paper, or scissors? (or quit)
?”
```

(Source: https://rosettacode.org/wiki/Rock-paper-scissors retrieved in December 2019.)

Now let's break down the code and discuss each step.

First, we import the random package which allows us to use several functions that we are going to take advantage of when giving the computer the ability to make random choices. Then we create a list for the three-game objects and print the game's rules so that the human player knows them. The computer will already know what to do because it is, after all, programmed. Next, we ask the player to type his or her choice, and then a loop is executed to check the choice of the player. The player also has the option of quitting the prompt window, and when that happens, the game is over. Our loop makes sure that if the player doesn't select the quit option, the game will run.

The next step is to ask the computer to select one of the three-game objects. This choice is done randomly, and the selected item is stored inside a variable called "computer." After the choice is memorized, the testing phase begins to see which player will win. First, a check is performed to see whether the two players have chosen the same item. If they did, then the result is a draw and nobody wins. Next, the program verifies whether the player chose rock, and then it looks at the computer to see if it chose scissors. If this is the case, since the rule says rock beats scissors, the player wins. If the computer didn't select a rock as well, neither did it pick scissors, then it certainly chose paper. In this case, the computer will win. Next, we have two "elif" statements where we perform two more tests that check whether the player selected paper or scissors. Here we also have a statement that checks to see if the player chose something that isn't one of the three possible items. If that is the case, an error message is sent that tells the player that they either chose something they are not allowed, or they mistyped the command.

Lastly, the user is prompted to type the next selection. This is where the main loop goes back to the beginning. In other words, the game starts with another round of rock, paper, scissors.

This game is simple, but it is fun because anyone can win. The computer has a chance of beating you, and there's also a real chance of ending up in a draw. Now that you understand how to create a random chance type of game, let's look at other examples to add to our game library while also learning Python programming.

Guess!

This project will be another fun chance-based game that will make use of the "random" module. The purpose of the game will be to choose a number between a minimum and a maximum, and then the opponent tries to guess that number. If the player guesses a higher number, they will have to try a smaller one, and the other way around as well. Only a perfect match will turn into a win.

We have also used the "input" function to interact with the program, and we are going to make use of it here once again. Besides, we will need a "while" loop as well.

In this project, the random module is needed because of certain specific functions. For instance, we know that we need to generate a random number; therefore, we will use a function called "randint" which stands for "random integer." The function will have two parameters, which represent the minimum number we can have, as well as the maximum. You can try out this function on its own. Just import the module and then type the following:

import random

```
random.randint (1, 20)
```

Python will now automatically generate a random figure between 1 and 20. Keep in mind that the minimum and maximum values are included in the number generation; therefore, Python can also generate numbers 1 or 20. You can test this command as many times as you want to make sure that you are truly getting random values. If you execute it often enough, you will see that some values will repeat themselves, and if the range is large enough, you might not even encounter certain numbers no matter how many times you run the code. What's interesting about this function though, is that it isn't truly random. This is just a side note that won't affect your program, but it is intriguing nonetheless. The "randint" function actually follows a specific pattern and the chosen numbers only appear to be random—but they aren't. Python follows a complex algorithm for this pattern instead, and therefore we experience the illusion of randomness. With that being said, let's get back to fun and games. Let's create our game with the following code:

```
import random

randomNumbers = random.randint (1, 100)

myGuess = int (input ("Try to guess the number. It can be anywhere from 1 to 100:"))

while guess != randomNumbers:

    if myGuess > randomNumbers:
```

```
        print (myGuess, "was larger than the number. Guess again!"

    if myGuess < randomNumbers:

        print (myGuess, "was smaller than the number. Guess again!"

myGuess = int (input ("Try and guess again! "))

print (myGuess, "you got it right! You won!")
```

That's it! Hopefully, you tried to create this game on your own because you already have the tools for the job. Remember that programming is only easy as long as you practice it enough on your own. Just take it one step at a time. With that being said, let's discuss the code in case you need some help figuring the game out:

Just like before, we first need to import the random module so that we can use the random number-generating function. Next, we use the "randint" function with two parameters. As mentioned before, these parameters are the lowest number we can guess, which is 1, and the highest number we can guess 100. The random number generator will give a number within this range. Once the number is generated, it is stored inside the "randomNumbers" variable we declared. This number will not be known by the player because he or she needs to guess it—that's the point of the game.

Next up, the player needs to guess the hidden number. This guess will then be stored inside a new variable called "myGuess." In order to check whether the guess is equal to the number, we are using a "while" loop with the "not equal to" operator. We do this because if the player gets lucky and guesses the number correctly with the first attempt, the loop simply doesn't finish executing because there's no need.

Next, if the player guesses the wrong number, we have two "if" statements that check whether the guess is a higher value than the hidden number, or a lower one. An appropriate message is then printed for the player to see in each case. In either scenario, the player receives another chance to make the right guess. Finally, if the user guessed the number correctly, the program declares victory by printing a message, and then the program stops running.

To make the game more interesting, you can challenge yourself to modify the random number generator to include different values. You can also add a statement that enables the game to print the score to see how many times the player tried to guess the number. Also, since the game ends when the player guesses, you could write the main loop so that the player can choose to restart the game instead of automatically quitting. Have fun and don't be afraid to try anything.

Conclusion

Thanks for purchasing/reading this book! I've learned a lot from writing it and I hope you have too.

Programming is a great skill to have. It's one of the fastest-growing jobs in the world, and it can make you money fast. However, it can seem like a big challenge, especially when it comes to how it's done. Many people have a vision of what they want to do with their lives and go about it in a certain way, but often they fail to achieve what they set out to do.

You might have a hard time getting started learning how to code. There are so many different languages that it can seem like there is no way that you can learn them all. The key to getting started is simply learning how to do it. You don't need to be a code monkey to become a successful programmer. All you need is interest and then the willingness to put in the time and effort.

The thing is, being a great coder doesn't have much to do with how smart you are or your education; it is more about the way you work and your ability to think outside the box. If you're looking for an easy-to-learn programming language, Python is a great option. It is one of the most popular programming languages, and it has a lot of great developers working with and on it.

This book will act as a guide if you are learning how to code in Python for the first time. This book was written for those who are completely new to programming and have no idea where to start.

Python is a great programming language for beginners that can be used for a lot of different things. It's easy to learn and easy to use, which makes it easy for someone who has no coding experience to pick up.

The book's structure is simple and very well designed. It covers everything from installing Python on your computer to downloading and installing modules and packages, as well as introducing you to "functions" and "classes." It explains everything step by step. It starts with the very basics of programming and finishes with more advanced topics.

Section one covered the principles of programming. When you're writing a program, it's not just about what goes in it; it's also about what comes out. The basic rules you need to learn to be a good programmer are covered, such as how to write a clean code.

The first principle of programming is that there's a problem to be solved. The second principle of programming is that there are many ways to solve the problem, and one way is not necessarily better than the other.

There are many different types of programming. The difference between all of them is how the code (programming) is structured and where it gets executed.

In section two of the book, you learned about Python, which is a programming language that's one of the most popular languages in use today. It is all about the actual programming.

Python is an open-source language, meaning anyone can take the source code and change it to make their own version of Python. Once you have your product or service, the next step is to develop a game that will draw people in.

While section three covered a step-by-step development of simple but intriguing games.

If you want to learn how to create games, don't expect the process to be easy. I would recommend the following steps when it comes to developing a game:

1. Stick to the core idea of what you want your game to be about.
2. Create a concept and character that people will connect with and relate to.

I sincerely hope you obtained the information you were seeking. If you enjoyed the book, then I've done my job. It's time to move onto the next stage of your journey and take action on the advice I've given you in this book.

The purpose of this book was to provide you with some content and information that can be useful for starting your programming journey. I hope it provided you with some insight into the programming field/industry and the inner workings of Python as one of the most popular programming language today.

As a programmer, you should always be asking yourself if you've done your job. You need to make sure that everything that you produce is worth the time and effort spent on it.

In the world of programming, there is no 'right' way to do it. The only way you can know what works best for you is by trial and error. You're just getting started, so it's important to remember that the journey of a thousand miles begins with a single first step. You must keep walking every single day after you take that first step.

As you progress in coding, the more you'll want to learn. I hope you will continue this learning process as you move forward in your career. Expose yourself to more of the different things in life and keep learning because that's how you can become even better at what you do.

Continuously practice the things you have learned and gather additional resources for a higher level of learning. You have a lot to learn, but that doesn't mean you can't start making progress. Your journey is just beginning. You haven't experienced much in life yet and you're still finding your way. So don't take yourself too seriously.

Printed in Great Britain
by Amazon

26084781R00079